# GRAFTING

# GRAFTING

Poems

AMY LUNDQUIST

*atmosphere press*

# Contents

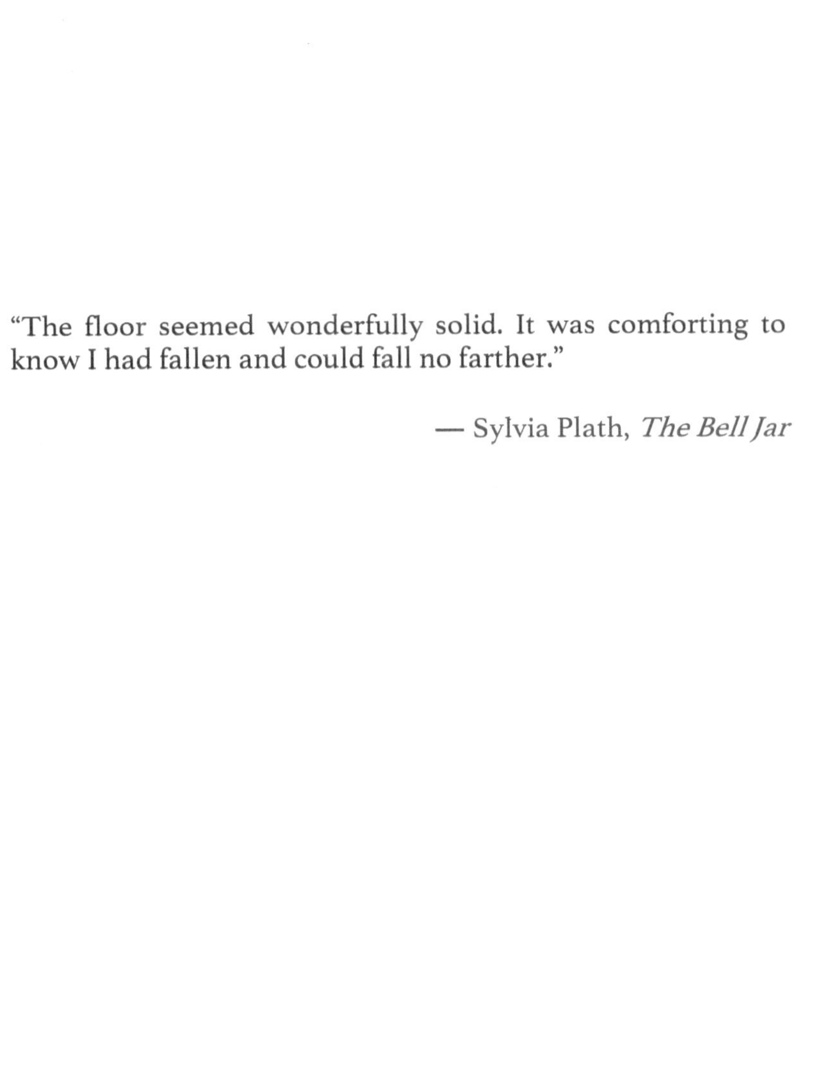

"The floor seemed wonderfully solid. It was comforting to know I had fallen and could fall no farther."

— Sylvia Plath, *The Bell Jar*

# Back To The Earth

Flay me open
at the spine.
Let me coat the cutting
board with tendons, guts, DNA.
Allow each moment
I've ever felt
collect in buckets
on the garage floor.
The dog will back away
at the stench
of my thoughts.

Let flies feed.

I desperately
need to be
an ounce
of nutrient for
a small flowering,
hand-grabbing,
wish-holding,
wind blowing,
prairie growing
dandelion.

# Facebook Wants Me To Be Friends With My Rapist

I look at him
and promise myself
that this is the last time
I ever have to see his face.

Ten years later,
Facebook wants me to know
that I might know him,
that we should connect,
because mutual acquaintances
mean friends.

His profile picture:
a small, petite
blonde-haired little girl
holding his hand.

# Molting

I started shedding
when I admitted
I was raped.

      Self-confidence.
         Happiness.
            Trust.
               Virginity.
                  Sexuality.

I spiraled toward vagueness,
hiding each layer
in the back of my closet.

A papier-mâché exterior
couldn't withstand my addiction
to peeling.

Attempting
a façade of purpose
and direction,
I became
opaque and hollow,
a single layer of flesh.

# Shame

My mind
has discovered
all the ways

        drank too much
        flirted too much
        recognized the intention
        spoke too softly

I can punish
myself for
being raped.

# Before, During, After

Picture this:
a small apartment
filled with friends,
noise levels hitting new heights.

Insert here:
cold drink in hand
cigarette pressed between lips
nineteen-year-old me dressed in vulnerability.

Flash to:
three a.m. stumbling to his bed
Did I whisper yes
through sloppy lips?

Wake up:
virginity lying on his floor
memories already fading out
I might puke.

# Day One

In my tiny dorm room,
I pull the shades
to keep out
the good morning sun.
The lights remain off
and I thank my roommate
for hating school
and leaving this weekend.

I undress and shove
my damaged clothes
under the bed,
gag at the smell
of the leftover fluids.

I am a dead pan body
and feel like Pig Pen,
from Charlie Brown,
dragging around
my poor choices;
a constant hazard.

# A Heart for A Heart

I push hard
through your flesh and muscle.
Feel every tendon snap
from my fingertips,
hanging limp off my hands
like the insides of a spaghetti squash.
Each rib splits and cracks
to make room for me,
like pushing my ass
through tight jeans.
I want to see
your eyes dilate
when my fingers grip
your heart and squeeze
it like a rotten orange.
When I pull out
from this excavation,

I want you

  to watch me

    devour it.

## A Few of Your Favorites

Every time I hear
Otis Redding,
I picture you
on the dock,
feet in the bay,
Captain & Coke in one hand,
Marlboro Red behind your ear,
and that bold
Bluefin Tuna t-shirt
starting at me
while I drown you.

# To My One and Only,

First off, fuck you.

Now, we can move on to the sentence of your crime. I will begin by removing each of your ten fingernails and ten toenails to remind you of the damage my hands and feet went through trying to climb out of the trauma you put me in. Let's watch the blood pool between your toes. I want to hear you beg for forgiveness. But I will ignore you; continue on by ripping your skin off, peeling your body like the husk on the corncobs of my childhood. Add some salt to the newborn flesh making sure each crevice is seasoned according to sensitivity. I will then pull you to my blacktopped driveway to leather under the sun. Don't worry; I'll be there with you, sitting under an umbrella, cold drink in my hand, waiting for the scavenger birds to feast off your freshly ruined body.

Love,
The girl you told everyone you fucked

# Paranormal Activity

I wake up late,
feel the memories crawl up
my spine and hunker
with darkness.

The presence of his body
still vivid in the sheets
the chalk outline
of a murder victim.

His pine and tobacco
scent lingers, hovering
above the bed
with an unfinished agenda.

I change the sheets
and move furniture
for better feng shei,
but the negative energy stays.

I abandon the room,
quarantine it from occupation
and rope off the entrance
with crime scene tape.

The house turns against me.

Each door is swollen
and warped, they
scream from the pain
of a forceful opening.

The toilet tank water
never stops running;
a constant irritant
instead of a lullaby.

I begin a ritual
of protection:

    Encrust skin in salt
    Encompass the body in sage smoke
    With a crystal outstretched, bow
    Acknowledge his apparition

The hauntings have become
immune to my rituals,
combating each defensive strike
with premonitions of suffering.

My ears ring
with echoes of voices
that mock my pleas
for forgiveness and acceptance.

My mind twists towards
fragmented memories
pushing my mental capacity
to insanity.

I am lost within
the dark hallways,
scramble toward every door
in order to let light in.

But I am cursed to live
within walls of this stranded,
haunted house, forced
to make it my home.

I try to forget.
I try to absolve.
I try to cleanse.
I try to pardon.

I am weak and need
an easy release,

so I give in
to darkness.

I shake hands with agonizing
nightmares, open windows
for more ghosts
to stretch and swell.

My desperation calls
for a séance in front
of the next blood moon.
"Prepare," it says,

"this rotation could
be the key
to relinquishing you
from this haunted home."

# Rapist

Men like you
should come with

a          **WARNING**          label
          stapled to your chest
          seared into your belly fat
          tattooed on your dick.
Because when you
decide to rape,
you should be scarred for life, too.

# Split

When a succulent's body
becomes leggy and tired
from stretching toward the sun,
the gardener takes
a pair of sharp shears
to cut between
the last open space
on the plant's stalk.

Separating two halves,
one is left aside
to squeeze all nutrients
from each petal and stem.
Relying only on itself
to regrow the root system—
an entirely new plant.

The original stalk is left
behind in the pot of soil,
bare boned and exposed.
Eventually
a callous builds over
the open wound,
beginning a journey
with a healthier chance
of reaching the sun.

# Imitation

Chorus of bees
humming and harvesting.
I am the mockingbird
trying to pass
for something much smaller
than nature made me.

# Lessons from the Venus Fly Trap

Allow him
to flatter
your obvious insecurities.
Watch closely
as he shows off
his prowess and masculinity.
Listen to stories
he blurts out
about each victory
lap he's run.
Wait patiently
for him to push his body
against yours.
When you feel his arrogance
move over you—

     S  N  A  P

        your jaw
        around him.
                Consume
                his warm body slowly.

# Depression

Leave everything.
Keep nothing.

# Allowance

Everything in me is convinced
time has run out.
The only thing I
have right is
these organs
no longer survive
in this shell.
Could this be
where my second wind
comes in?
What happens when you have
already used your
second, third, fifth, thirteenth
wind given?
Are you allowed a thirty-first?

# Cope

When my mind becomes
an abandoned cave
with decomposed memories,
I shout, "HEY!"
and listen to my voice
echo through empty caverns.

When my pulse and thoughts
pick up speed
in a crowded venue,
I retreat
into myself
like an armadillo.

And when my body feels
like an overstretched,
rotted rubber band
about to snap,
I seek solace
in mortality.

# Knock, Knock

She enjoys
making me weep,
pushing at the soft
spots of my heart,
poking at my lack
of confidence,
tears are at the edge.
In order to stop
water from cascading
over the dam,
I pinch soft, tender
skin of my underarm
or thigh or bite my cheek
—hard—
trying to reinforce
the patched up foundation.
There's short relief.
But she always
picks up the hammer
to remind me
she's not ready to leave.

# Tell Me

when the day will arrive
that releases me
of every expectation,
because
I'm tired of the demands.
I'm tired of the desires.
I'm exhausted from trying
to fit myself
into myself.

# Letting Go

I can't apologize
to myself—
even if
I could—
I would not willingly
offer forgiveness.

# About Me

One.
I like my coffee black and hot even when it's summer. I love cereal and would eat it for every meal if I were allowed to. I don't like conflict and am always willing to swallow my feelings quickly, like a shot of bad whiskey, just to make everyone around me comfortable. And I have this notion that I must be perfect so then I won't get in trouble and everyone will like me and I'll always agree with you because it's the easy way out of a discussion. I'm especially great at pretending to be who I think you want me to be. But now, I can't seem to find my way back to myself and I've become a collage of personalities, none of them genuine. My belly is boiling over all my regressed emotions and    SHIT!
        all I want is to not be scared of my own mind.

Two.
This week's only attention worthy headline:
*Girls fought back after teen boys rated them on looks.*

Three.
I'm an Aries and according to my Witchy friend, I am "totally an Aries". She tells me that on my 30th birthday, there is a New Moon. Apparently that means big things are going to happen during this year's Slow Skate at the roller rink of my life. But what she doesn't know is that reaching this birthday is a milestone, not because it's 30, but because I thought that Depression and Mars were scheming to stop me at twenty-nine.

# A Consideration

When I die,
I leave
each of my
tragedies and triumphs.
This could satisfy
the craving I have
never been able
to identify.

# Nature's Response

Two A.M.
I'm awake
because the stars
won't stop gossiping
about the latest
cosmic love story.
I'm begging
Moon for advice
but she only tells me,
*go.*

I left
my comforts, walked
toward the beach,
hoping Ocean
had convinced Moon
to give up answers.
The tide began
grazing my feet and ankles
with warm saltwater, sand
started filling gaps
between toes.
Ocean continued his pursuit
by swallowing thighs with soft
waves, manipulating each motion
around waist, chest,
lulling me with consistent finesse.
Closing eyes,
my head rolls back.
He rounds shoulders,
follows curves to my neck,
gently kissing nape, lips, ears.
He takes lungs
and Moon whispers,
*relax; you're safe now.*

# I've Never Been Good at Math

Somehow solving
*x multiplied by y minus twenty-nine*
will solve the chemical
imbalance in my body
and the days my lungs
can't hold enough
oxygen or ones that seem
longer than twenty-four hours,
I consider if
it would be better
for me to swallow
the whole pill
bottle and take myself
out of the equation.

# Suicide

Why do we consider
suicide selfish?
Many believe to kill
a suffering animal
to be a noble act.
Is human pain
not worthy
of such compassion?

# Tricks

The eight-foot walls
of my bedroom
escalade to
nine feet
ten feet
twelve feet.

Forcing the perspective
out of bounds.

fifteen feet
eighteen feet
twenty-five feet

My hands reach
to grasp anything
to steady me,
but they can't grip.
They can't halt momentum
from dragging me down.

I wake up
to a sweaty pillow.
Leap out of my bed
like it's a pit of cockroaches.
I glare at it.
Disgusted that I've been lied to.
There's no solace here,
no comfort within the sheets.

*

The next night I'm
wishing for stability.
My lids close,
walls shoot up
twenty-eight feet

thirty feet
thirty-three feet.
My hands slip
down smooth surfaces.
I force open my eyes,
alert myself to reality,
but the walls keep
skyrocketing.
The void expands
and vacuums all
oxygen in my lungs.
thirty-four feet
forty feet
forty-eight feet.

*

Cup after cup after cup of coffee leads to glass after glass
after glass of wine leads to [inhale, hold, exhale] after [inhale,
hold, exhale] after [inhale, hold, exhale]; my new routine of
tricks my body plays on my mind.

*

The third night,
fifty feet
fifty-five feet
sixty-three feet.
I'm awake,
sixty-five feet
seventy feet
eighty-two feet.

*

Logically, I conclude
that sleeping is no
longer safe.

*

Class begins. Dark theater. Citizen Kane on screen. The camera scans a room stuffed with fancy furniture and trinkets, it pans toward a man lying on a couch with a snow globe in his hand. Camera zooms toward the snow globe.

It's getting bigger.

The snow globe is getting closer.

Instinctively my hands shoot outward.

Press PAUSE on the falling snow globe.

The theater feels like a blanket over my head, an obstruction over my mouth.

My mental comprehension breaks.

Flee. Flee. Flee. Flee.Flee.FleeFleeFleeFlee.

GET OUT OF HERE

I'm weeping on my speed walk home, thinking about being trapped in a continuous loop of my surroundings swallowing me.

My hands can't save me.

# Six-Month Check-Up

My dentist tells me that I clench my jaw and grind my teeth when I sleep. She says it's so bad that my molars and K-9s are almost flat. I wish to tell her that my jaw and my sleep are where I hold all my anxiety but I keep quiet and nod because even with her fingers and tools in my mouth, she won't understand. She then tells me that I brush too aggressively, the enamel is disappearing; I can't get it back. I want to explain that it's because I've been spending extensive time trying to scrub away the bitter leftovers of men from my mouth. I've been taking hotter, longer showers to scorch any piece of remembrance of my mistakes. Scrubbing the skin hard so that I can peel off freckles and watch them swirl down the drain. My nails are frequently clipped short, no chance of growth. I've been letting my hair grow long, leaving the ends split and dead. My body is now a dilapidated structure with no foundation to build upon. And my teeth—my mouth—happen to be another part of my body I am desperately trying to cleanse. My enamel and sharpened molars are more errors I can add to my list called: "Qualities I Will Never See Again". But she doesn't care and she doesn't need to know, so again, I nod, and mentally add these items to my list called: "Conversations for my Therapist".

# Trace

Small cut
above my knee,
pick off the flaky
dried scab,
observe liquid hemoglobin
seep out.
I show myself,
with empirical evidence,

I'm alive.
I'm alive.
I'm alive.

# Let Us Be Dust

I watched my dreams spontaneously combust last night over dinner. The ashes fell on the mashed potatoes, half-eaten steak, and filled the empty space my peas inhabited before I ate them. Maybe it was the way the peas mixed with my stomach acid that fueled the combustion, or maybe it was the density that filled the air.

I pushed my chair back from the small oak table. The cat tried to sift through the remains with her paw. I scooted her back with my foot, grabbed the broom and dustpan, and collected all my dreams' particles. With a pile on the tile floor, I looked for a vase to put them in, to make it seem like they were cremated. I want to reincarnate my dreams as a bookend. But I couldn't find a vase anywhere in the house. Instead, I watched the particles sink to the bottom of the fishbowl. I always wanted sand in the bottom of it.

## Stale

I sat in my car outside my friend's house. There is stillness in here that I have never heard before. The car keys felt dense against my clammy palm. I looked out the window and saw her neighbor's kids playing tag. Their laughs were muffled in this contained atmosphere. I lifted my hand to the door handle but decided on this stillness instead.

I stared down at my shoes and noticed how they didn't look black enough, same with my dress. It was like the sun had faded them both in the fifteen minutes it took me to drive to her house. I wish she were here to tell me they're fine. I wish she could see how her Dad got the grass to be so green this summer. I wish she hadn't left me here in this claustrophobic car. I wish she had waited to see what tomorrow brought.

# Unwanted Friendship

Fourteen years old.
Spanish class.
Suicide took the
desk next to mine.

She answered
every question correctly.
Homework
always finished.
Her curly black hair
perfectly parted down
the middle of her scalp.

I hated her.

She showed up every day wearing
bell-bottom, low-rise jeans with
black Etnies skate shoes.
She strutted down the hall
when she wore her black shirt
with the long-sleeved fish net top over it,
always showing just the acceptable amount
of midriff to slide by
the School Dress Code Policy undetected.

Fifteen years later,
her and I sit
cross-legged in my closet
counting
each
and
every
pill from the prescribed bottle
and arguing about how many
I would have to take
in order to see the friend
who occupied the desk next to mine.

# Weeping Willow

I imagine
your limbs grow
long, downward
because your roots
absorb every piece
of sadness humans
leak from our feet.

When each gust of wind
tosses your leaves,
you slip each
ounce of trauma
into the breeze,
releasing it from
your grasp.

You cleanse your mind
more beautifully than
we do ours.

Stay steady, Willow.
We need you
to carry this load.

# Renewed

Pour a thin layer
of lavender Epsom salts
on the bottom of the bathtub.
Fill the entirety
of it with hot water.
Hot enough to make pale
flesh red like a lobster
in a boiling pot.
Marinate the meat
of my body
in Cabernet Sauvignon,
bold, complex, deep notes of oak.
Saturate myself until
the pruning skin
begins to peel away,
revealing the soft
tenderness of fresh
material, ready to be
dried and calloused.

# Alterations

She's a hand
painted, one-of-a-kind paper
doll, barely played with.

She's constructed from thin
basic paper, shoulders
slightly rounded
from living in an envelope
in the bottom desk drawer,
clothes have slight tears
and creases in them,
worn but still stiff.

The first boy
got a hold of her
and was too aggressive,
ripped her almost
all the way across
her heart.
With damage
done quickly,
he cast her into a box
labeled "give-away".

The second boy
found her damaged body
and stripped her down
to her underwear—
convinced he knew
what she really needed.
Her sexless panties and bra
didn't entice him enough.
He tried to contort
another paper doll's
lacey lingerie to attach
but it didn't work,
she looked awkward

trying to wear something
that wasn't hers.

The third boy
gave her a piece
of tape to mend her body,
softened her up
with acceptance
of her journey,
then slowly twisted
his acceptance into
demands, constantly
pushing for more.

After the third boy
threw her out,
she fumbled from hands to hands
but eventually landed back
in her original envelope
away from all attention.
She came to accept
the worn body she now had.
She accepted
that she'll forever be
this paper doll,
unable to conform
to any other shape.

# Midnight Confessions

We swapped
trauma reports
as if we were kids
telling ghost stories.

We took
long, soft pulls
on Newport cigarettes
between vivid
depiction of a man's
hand inching up
your thirteen-year-old leg,
unbuttoning your pants,
and extracting each piece
of childhood left
in your pre-teen body.

We took
chasers of cheap beer
in order to choke down
the documentary recap
of my immature body
being pillaged.

We made
quiet, tender glances
as we watched each other
pick sore, unhealed scabs
until they bled.

We attempted
to bandage them with
a mutual understanding
of extinguished trust.

But there would be
no submission to anyone.

# Bad Advice

There he was—
five feet eleven inches,
vegetarian fueled,
earth saving,
book loving man—
standing in front of me.
His soft voice
whispered an escape route
from the swamp
I was submerged in.

The sweetness of
his brown sugar eyes
folded me into a distorted
version of understanding.
I allowed him
to take me,
but when the zipper
of my vulnerability
jammed and body
seized under the flashback,
I pushed him off.

While my mind
desperately grasped
to mute the flurry
of panic,

I heard him,

"Come on.
Don't stop."

# Shape-Shifting

When I was young,
people used to tell me
I wouldn't always
be skinny—
two McChickens,
medium fries, extra sweet
& sour sauce would become
my thighs,
the size zero
low-rise jeans
wouldn't contain my hips,
and the
lack of forgiveness
would become my ass.

Now that I've arrived
at this body-altering,
metabolism-slowing,
place in my life,
I believe my thighs
have grown only to
store each piece of
my depression,
my hips simply need
more jean space
to hold all my regrets,
and my ass
has only grown in size
to soften the fall
every time
I trip over my heart.

My body has developed
new ways to wear
my emotions
beside my sleeve.

# An Ode to the Women Who Didn't Keep Quiet

I hear you
        during your statement to
                your therapist
                your partner
                your best friend
                your parents
                Congress
                the press

I believe you
        during the questioning about
                how much you drank
                what you were wearing
                if you went to a doctor
                if you remember flirting
                if you leaned in to kiss first
                if you told anyone

I stand with you
        while you can't stop
                the whispering about you
                the suicidal plans
                shame to build in your gut
                a barricade from erecting around you
                self-hate from consuming your thoughts
                everyone from finding out

# Move On

If this tragedy can't dwell
on my tongue,
where would be
an acceptable
place to put it?

How about I
bury it in the backyard
next to the decaying
hamster I had
when I was ten?

Should I take
it out for ice cream
and break up over
waffle cones? Let
it down easy?

What if I cram
it down the sink
with other scraps
to be pulverize
in the disposal?

Maybe, I should sell it
to the neighbor kid
like I did
with that bag
of weed I didn't
want to be found.

How old do I
have to be
before I get
to decide what
is worth sharing?

# Trust

Naked bodies
pressed together,
my heart
transfers into yours.

## Taking Notes

Last night,
we laid under
the sheets on your bed,
you over me,
kissing every nook
and cranny my body offered,
I began to wonder
if you kissed her
with such heat and desire.
I wondered if you felt
the same necessity to touch
her as you do with me.
Do I occupy her side
of your bed better?
Does my body fit
alongside yours easier?
Where do I rank higher
and fall short?
I wish to be
a better lover than her.
I wish to be
her opposite,
remind you of everything
but her.
I wish you will hold on
to me far longer
than you did with her.
I wish this time
when I say,
"I love you,"
I actually mean it.

# Health & Wellness

I try to convince
myself, that what you
did to me is like having a bruise:
soft, sore, several shades of purple,
an injury that eventually heals.

I can't stop
pressing it every
moment I'm alone, keeping
it consistently throbbing
like a clock's ticking.

I'm attempting to accept
the severity of damage
you inflicted upon me.

I can recover.

# Publications

"Six-Month Check-Up" published by: Eastern Iowa Review in Issue 10

Earlier version of "Facebook Wants Me to Be Friends with My Rapist" published by: For Women Who Roar in Volume 3: Still Healing Part 1

# About Atmosphere Press

Atmosphere Press is an independent, full-service publisher for excellent books in all genres and for all audiences. Learn more about what we do at atmospherepress.com.

We encourage you to check out some of Atmosphere's latest releases, which are available at Amazon.com and via order from your local bookstore:

*The Unordering of Days,* poetry by Jessica Palmer

*It's Not About You,* poetry by Daniel Casey

*A Dream of Wide Water,* poetry by Sharon Whitehill

*Radical Dances of the Ferocious Kind*, poetry by Tina Tru

*The Woods Hold Us,* poetry by Makani Speier-Brito

*My Cemetery Friends: A Garden of Encounters at Mount Saint Mary in Queens, New York*, nonfiction and poetry by Vincent J. Tomeo

*Report from the Sea of Moisture,* poetry by Stuart Jay Silverman

*The Enemy of Everything*, poetry by Michael Jones

*The Stargazers,* poetry by James McKee

*The Pretend Life*, poetry by Michelle Brooks

*Minnesota and Other Poems*, poetry by Daniel N. Nelson

## About the Author

Amy Lundquist earned her BFA in Creative Writing from the University of North Carolina Wilmington. She has been published in: Atlantis: UNCW Creative Magazine, Charlotte Viewpoint, Her Heart Poetry, For Women Who Roar, and Eastern Iowa Review. Amy currently resides in St. Paul, MN. She lives with her husband, dog, and three cats. You can follow her here:

Instagram: @amy.lundquist.poetry
Twitter: @amylundquist2
http://amylundquistpoetry.squarespace.com/